EFFECTIVE TRADE UNIONISM

By James Connolly

Introduction by
Liam McNulty
Sean Matgamna

Edited by Sean Matgamna

Effective Trade Unionism, *by James Connolly*

Introduction by Liam McNulty, Sean Matgamna

More publications at workersliberty.org/publications

Contact us or get involved:

workersliberty.org

awl@workersliberty.org

020 7394 8923

20E Tower Workshops
Riley Road
London SE1 3DG

fb.com/workersliberty
twitter.com/workersliberty
instagram.com/workersliberty
youtube.com/c/WorkersLibertyUK

Edited by Sean Matgamna
Printed by Imprint Digital
Exeter
EX5 5HY

ISBN: 978-1-909639-62-1

Contents

Labor

Berton Braley

Out of chaos, out of murk
I arose and did my work
While the ages changed and sped
I was toiling for my bread
Underneath my sturdy blows
Forests fell and cities rose.
And the hard, reluctant soil
Blossomed richly from my toil.
Palaces and temples grand
Wrought I with my cunning hand.
Rich indeed was my reward —
Stunted soul, and body scarred
With the marks of scourge and rod
I, the tiller of the sod.
From the cradle to the grave
Shambled through the world — a slave!
Crushed and trampled, beaten, cursed,
Serving best, but served the worst,
Starved and cheated, gouged and spoiled.
Still I builded, still I toiled,
Undernourished, underpaid
In the world myself had made.

Up from slavery I rise,
Dreams and wonder in my eyes.
After brutal ages past
Coming to my own at last
I was slave — but I am free!
I was blind — but I can see!
I, the builder, I, the maker,
I, the calm tradition-breaker,
Slave and serf and clod no longer,
Know my strength — and who is stronger?
I am done with ancient frauds,
Ancient lies and ancient gods —
All that sham is overthrown,
I shall take and keep my own.
Unimpassioned, unafraid,
Master of the World I've made!

Introduction

Wanting a road from capitalism to socialism, James Connolly sought, experimented, groped in a number of different organisations.

With Jim Larkin, Connolly led the workers' side in the 1913 Dublin Labour War. He went from Secretary of the Irish Transport and General Workers' Union to be military commander of the insurgents of Dublin in 1916, and from that, on 12 May 1916, to a seat — he had a leg wound turned gangrenous — before a British Army firing squad in the killing yard of Kilmainham Jail.

Some of his ideas have to be criticised now, such as his ideas about ancient Irish society, but to one idea he clung from the turn of the century to his death in 1916 — industrial unionism, workers' solidarity across grades and trades, and sympathetic strikes. That is how he saw his work with Larkin on the Irish Transport Union: a union for an industry and the members watching the moment until they could take over running the industry.

I

Connolly at first followed a socialist consensus which he would later summarise like this:

> *"If it were now possible to examine the socialist speeches of that period we would find that an inordinately large proportion of time was given up in them to a belittling of industrial action and to what was practically an exaggeration of the ease and facility with which the working class could achieve its rights at the ballot-box."*
>
> — *"Changes",* Forward, *9 May 1914*

He did not disdain trade unions even then. He was a member of the Dublin United Labourers' Union, and represented this body on Dublin Trades Council. The union, in turn, sponsored Connolly's electoral contest in the Wood Quay ward of Dublin Corporation in March 1902.

His strategic views changed in the early years of the twentieth century as Connolly embraced the views of Daniel De Leon.

He became a De Leon man at the turn of the century. And in his conception of his union work he remained a De Leonite long after he broke with De Leon the man.

Daniel De Leon (1852-1914) was the leader of the Socialist Labor Party (SLP) of the USA and of a small group of smaller Socialist Labor Parties in Britain and a few other countries. All of them were in the Second (Socialist) International, which allowed for more than one affiliate in a single country.

De Leon ran the SLP-USA very rigidly, and they were hostile to all of the other socialists. At that time the only US unions, in the American Federation of Labor led by Sam Gompers, could accurately be described as "lily-white job trusts", effectively business unions which aspired only to organise the elite of the working class and barred black and Chinese workers.

In 1905 in Chicago, De Leon united with Eugene Debs, a leader of the railway workers, Big Bill Haywood, a leader of the Western Federation of Miners, and others to form the Industrial Workers of the World (IWW) as a revolutionary union organisation open to all.

They were known as the Wobblies. Ironically, because wobbly is the last thing they were. The way they got the name was typical of them. A Chinese member could only say he was a member of the I Wobble Wobble, so they took the name Wobbly and bore it proudly as a badge of honour.

The IWW split in 1908, the De Leonists on one side and the working-class trade unionists and some socialists on the other. James Connolly became an organiser for Eugene Debs's Socialist Party, and then for the majority IWW. All of them kept the policy of industrial unionism, but it was De Leon who had theorised it.

The bourgeoisie under feudalism had control of trade and towns. They controlled a part of the division of labour in society. They took centuries to develop their own wealth and strength. Therefore, they could take power when they were acting under false religious beliefs. They already had much of society's wealth.

Unlike the bourgeoisie, the working class remains the basic wage-slave class in society. It does not combine political subordination with control of a part of the means of production or of society's surplus wealth. The nearest thing we have to our own "organic" intellectuals is the trade union officials. The working class must take power deliberately, knowingly, consciously, in one combined movement. This is the fundamental problem of the working class as a revolutionary class.

II

James Connolly expressed it plainly at the beginning of an article he wrote in America after he had broken with De Leonist party.

> *"There is not a Socialist in the world today who can indicate with any degree of clearness how we can bring about the co-operative commonwealth except along the lines suggested by industrial organisation of the workers"*
>
> — *"Industrial Unionism and Constructive Socialism"*

All the industrial unionists, in the first place in terms of clarity the De Leonists, argued that the working class must build in every industry "one big union". This union must correspond to the given industry, be an understudy (so to speak) for the controlling capitalists, and be ready as a signal to take over the industry.

The bourgeoisie had its own intellectuals and its own systems of thought within feudalism. The working class must have its own party, taking care of politics and all the problems of leading the industrial unions and of industrial society.

As Connolly saw it, this conception linked the broad social aim with the immediate class struggle. It also "destroys at one blow all the fears of a bureaucratic State, ruling and ordering the lives of every individual from above, and thus gives assurance that the social order of the future will be an extension of the freedom of the individual": it was his answer to Hilaire Belloc's claim that social reform and social provision would produce "the servile state".

Other people who did not know or who failed to understand De Leon supported industrial unions. This trend, sometimes called syndicalism, became a powerful movement in many countries, including Britain, in the years before World War One. The syndicalists expected to take power in society, and soon.

Larkin, and then James Connolly, thought were building an industrial union in the Irish Transport Workers Union. They were not apolitical syndicalists. In 1912 and after the unions founded a Labour Party (the "Irish Trades Union Congress and Labour Party"; they became separate organisations in 1930).

Powerful syndicalist movements would surge across Britain in the 1970s. There were some 200 workplace occupations in those years.

The difference was that the syndicalists before 1914 believed that what they did in industry was an active, direct preparation for socialism. The 1970s syndicalists had no such perspective. They voted Labour or, disproportionately, Communist Party.

A central flaw in the syndicalist reasoning was that the big unions became bureaucratised, too, perhaps more, or more easily, than the old craft unions.

III

Connolly worked for the industrial unionist conception from when he became a De Leonist early in the 20th century. When he broke with De Leon personally, he did not break with the idea of the Big Industrial Union.

He lived long enough and gained enough experience, notably in the Dublin Labour war of 1913-14, to see (in the article, "Old Wine in New Bottles") what was wrong with the syndicalist conception, and he even identified wildcat strikes as a partial answer to bureaucratisation. Not long enough to see how the Russian revolution developed workers' councils, alongside unions, as both vehicles of struggle in revolutionary times and modes of workers' rule, while retaining independent trade unions as a safeguard.

The Dublin Labour War of 1913-14 is one of the great epics of working class struggle and endeavour. Officially, it lasted from August 1913 to mid-January 1914, but some of the lockouts dragged on beyond that date.

It is well known throughout the world because Vladimir Lenin wrote about it. That was in the first week, and therefore, many of his judgements were not true for the strike-lockout as a whole. Nor were the locked out workers innocents picked upon by the 400 Dublin employers who banded together to fight them. The Dublin workers who were members of Jim Larkin's union, the Irish Transport and General Workers' Union, really had provoked the employers. They really had banded together and used sympathetic, or solidarity, strikes so that no small workplace was isolated in its struggles, and every group could appeal to workers indirectly involved in their trade to back them.

Seafarers could depend on Dublin dockers to strike until the seafarers were allowed to join their Union. Union members would act on behalf of or in alliance with other embattled workers.

Many rural workers came to Dublin for employment, thus pushing wages down. The union and solidarity action exerted pressure in the opposite direction. Slowly, the wages of general labourers were pushed up.

Solidarity strikes have been illegal in Britain since the 1980s. Labour leader Tony Blair expressed the idea that Britain had the most repressive labour laws in Western Europe, but as Labour prime minister he did not remove the Thatcher anti-union laws. Neither did his successor, Gordon Brown. Their removal remains something for the labour movement to achieve in the future.

In Dublin, the successes of sympathy-strike action led to the lockout and strike. Coordinated by an elderly Dublin millionaire reprobate, William Martin Murphy, the employers hit back. Connolly described the scene early on the conflict.

"Take the case of the United Builders Labourers' Trade Union, for instance.

This was a rival union to the Irish Transport Workers' Union. Many sharp passages had occurred between them, and the employers counted confidently upon their cooperation in the struggle...

"When the members of their union were asked to sign the agreement [demanded by the bosses], promising never to join or help the Transport Union, not one man consented — but all over Dublin their 2,500 members marched out 'to help the Transport boys'...

"What is true of that union is also true of most of the tradesmen. All are showing wonderful loyalty to their class. Coachbuilders, sawyers, engineers, bricklayers, each trade that is served by general labourers, walks out along with the Transport boys; refuses to even promise to work with any one who signs the employers' agreement, and, cheering, lines up along with their class.

"Or think of the heroic women and girls. Did they care to evade the issue, they might have remained at work, for the first part of the agreement asks them to merely repudiate the Transport Workers, and as women they are members of the Irish Women Workers' Union, not of the Transport.

"But the second part pledges them to refuse to 'help' the Transport Union — and in every shop, factory and sweating hell-hole in Dublin, as the agreement is presented, they march out with pinched faces, threadbare clothes, and miserable footgear, but with high hopes, undaunted spirit, and glorious resolve shining out of their eyes."

The British labour movement backed Dublin heroically, sending money. Ships full of food sent by the labour movement to support the strikers and locked-out workers steamed into Dublin repeatedly. The power of the bosses to compel workers by starving their children was severely limited. Much of Dublin was tied up.

Magnificent as British labour movement help in food and money was, it was not enough. Only strikes in solidarity with Dublin could have inflicted the necessary damage on the Dublin employers. A class struggle like that of Dublin has a logic of its own. The logic of the strike-lockout in Dublin, and of British labour movement help to the Dublin workers, was a general strike in the UK.

Militants in Britain took up the call for a General Strike. The idea was seriously discussed for the first time since Chartist times (there had been a General Strike in 1842 in the North of England, the so named Plug Riots).

But the union officials fought it off. They drew the line at strikes in support of Dublin. The long, unequal struggle dragged on.

In January the Irish leaders called on Dublin workers to go back on the best terms they could get. The bosses hadn't won. The union survived. But the workers hadn't won either. The power of the workers had been curtailed, for a while.

IV

The experiments in socialism and trade unionism of Connolly's time will go on because socialism is the alternative to exploitation, and wage slavery goes on. We learn from our setbacks and defeats. Rosa Luxemburg said it provokingly but well:

> *"Revolution is the only form of 'war'... in which the ultimate victory can be prepared only by a series of 'defeats'.*
>
> *"What does the entire history of socialism and of all modern revolutions show us? The first spark of class struggle in Europe, the revolt of the silk weavers in Lyon in 1831, ended with a heavy defeat; the Chartist movement in Britain ended in defeat; the uprising of the Parisian proletariat in the June days of 1848 ended with a crushing defeat; and the Paris Commune ended with a terrible defeat.*
>
> *"The whole road of socialism — so far as revolutionary struggles are concerned — is paved with nothing but thunderous defeats... Where would we be today without those 'defeats', from which we draw historical experience, understanding, power and idealism?... We stand on the foundation of those very defeats... because each one contributes to our strength and understanding"*

The end of Russian and European Stalinism frees the working class. Whatever is new, whatever the working class invents, it is certain that it will centre around working class solidarity and combativity, the virtues which James Connolly surveys, chronicles, facilitates, and explains in these articles about Effective Trade Unionism.

The texts in this booklet have been checked against the originals. In some cases this is the first reprinting since they originally appeared; in others, cuts in previous reprintings have been made good.

Industrial Unionism and Constructive Socialism

"There is not a Socialist in the world today who can indicate with any degree of clearness how we can bring about the co-operative commonwealth except along the lines suggested by industrial organisation of the workers.

"Political institutions are not adapted to the administration of industry. Only industrial organisations are adapted to the administration of a co-operative commonwealth that we are working for. Only the industrial form of organisation offers us even a theoretical constructive Socialist programme. There is no constructive Socialism except in the industrial field".

The above extracts from the speech of Delegate Stirton, editor of the *Wage Slave*, of Hancock, Michigan, so well embody my ideas upon this matter that I have thought well to take them as a text for an article in explanation of the structural form of Socialist Society. In a previous chapter I have analysed the weakness of the craft or trade union form of organisation alike as a weapon of defence against the capitalist class in everyday conflict on the economic field, and as a generator of class consciousness on the political field, and pointed out the greater effectiveness for both purposes of an industrial form of organisation.

In the present article I desire to show how they who are engaged in building up industrial organisations for the practical purpose of today are at the same time preparing the framework of the society of the future. It is the realisation of that fact that indeed marks the emergence of Socialism as a revolutionary force from the critical to the positive stage. Time was when Socialists, if asked how society would be organised under Socialism, replied invariably, and airily, that such things would be left to the future to decide. The fact was that they had not considered the matter, but the development of the Trust and organised Capital in general, making imperative the Industrial Organisations of Labour on similar lines, has provided us with an answer at once more complete to ourselves and more satisfying to our questioners.

Now to analyse briefly the logical consequences of the position embodied in the above quotation.

"Political institutions are not adapted to the administration of industry." Here is a statement that no Socialist with a clear knowledge of the essentials of his doctrine can dispute. The political institutions of today are simply the coercive forces of capitalist society they have grown up out of, and are based upon, territorial divisions of power in the hands of the ruling class in past ages, and were carried over into capitalist society to suit the needs of the capitalist class when that class overthrew the dominion of its predecessors.

The delegation of the function of government into the hands of representatives elected from certain districts, States or territories, represents no real natural division suited to the requirements of modern society, but is a survival from a time when territorial influences were more potent in the world than industrial influences, and for that reason is totally unsuited to the needs of the new social order, which must be based upon industry.

The Socialist thinker, when he paints the structural form of the new social order, does not imagine an industrial system directed or ruled by a body of men or women elected from an indiscriminate mass of residents within given districts, said residents working at a heterogeneous collection of trades and industries. To give the ruling, controlling, and directing of industry into the hands of such a body would be too utterly foolish.

What the Socialist does realise is that under a Social Democratic form of society the administration of affairs will be in the hands of representatives of the various industries of the nation; that the workers in the shops and factories will organise themselves into unions, each union comprising all the workers at a given industry; that said union will democratically control the workshop life of its own industry, electing all foremen etc., and regulating the routine of labour in that industry in subordination to the needs of society in general, to the needs of its allied trades, and to the departments of industry to which it belongs; that representatives elected from these various departments of industry will meet and form the industrial administration or national government of the country.

In short, Social Democracy, as its name implies, is the application to industry, or to the social life of the nation, of the fundamental principles of democracy. Such application will necessarily have to begin in the workshop, and proceed logically and consecutively upward through all the grades of industrial organisation until it reaches the culminating point of national executive power and direction. In other words, Social Democracy must proceed from the bottom upward, whereas capitalist political society is organised from above downward; Social democracy will be administered by a committee of experts elected from the industries and professions of the land; capitalist society is governed by representatives elected from districts, and is based upon territorial division.

The local and national governing, or rather administrative, bodies of Socialists will approach every question with impartial minds, armed with the fullest expert knowledge born of experience; the governing bodies of capitalist society have to call in an expensive professional expert to instruct them on every technical question, and know that the impartiality of said expert varies with, and depends upon, the size of his fee.

It will be seen that this conception of Socialism destroys at one blow all the fears of a bureaucratic State, ruling and ordering the lives of every individual from above, and thus gives assurance that the social order of the future will be an extension of the freedom of the individual, and not the suppression of it. In short, it blends the fullest democratic control with the most absolute expert supervision, something unthinkable of any society built upon the political State.

To focus the idea properly in your mind you have but to realise how industry today transcends all limitations of territory and leaps across rivers, mountains and continents; then you can understand how impossible it would be to apply to such far-reaching intricate enterprises the principle of democratic control by the workers through the medium of political territorial divisions.

Under Socialism, States, territories, or provinces will exist only as geographical expressions, and have no existence as sources of governmental power, though they may be seats of administrative bodies.

Now, having grasped the idea that the administrative force of the Socialist republic of the future will function through unions industrially organised, that the principle of democratic control will operate through the workers correctly organised in such Industrial Unions, and that the political territorial State of capitalist society will have no place or function under Socialism, you will at once grasp the full truth embodied in the words of this member of the Socialist Party whom I have just quoted, that "only the industrial form of organisation offers us even a theoretical constructive Socialist programme."

To some minds constructive Socialism is embodied in the work of our representatives on the various public bodies to which they have been elected. The various measures against the evils of capitalist property brought forward by, or as a result of, the agitation of Socialist representatives on legislative bodies are figured as being of the nature of constructive Socialism.

As we have shown, the political State of capitalism has no place under Socialism; therefore, measures which aim to place industries in the hands of, or under the control of, such a political State are in no sense steps towards that ideal; they are but useful measures to restrict the greed of capitalism and to familiarise the workers with the conception of common ownership. This latter is, indeed, their chief function.

But the enrolment of the workers in unions patterned closely after the structure of modern industries, and following the organic lines of industrial development, is par excellence the swiftest, safest, and most peaceful form of constructive work the Socialist can engage in. It prepares within the framework of capitalist society the working forms of the Socialist republic, and thus, while increasing the resisting power of the worker against present encroachments of the capitalist class, it familiarises him with the idea that the union he is helping to build up is destined to supplant that class in the control of the industry in which he is employed.

The power of this idea to transform the dry detail work of trade union organisation into the constructive work of revolutionary Socialism, and thus make of the unimaginative trade unionist a potent factor in the launching of a new system of society, cannot be over-estimated. It invests the sordid details of the daily incidents of the class struggle with a new and beautiful meaning, and presents them in their true light as skirmishes between the two opposing armies of light and darkness.

In the light of this principle of industrial unionism every fresh shop or factory organised under its banner is a fort wrenched from the control of the capitalist class and manned with the soldiers of the revolution to be held by them for the workers.

On the day that the political and economic forces of Labour finally break with capitalist society and proclaim the Workers' Republic, these shops and factories so manned by industrial unionists will be taken charge of by the workers there employed, and force and effectiveness be thus given to that proclamation. Then and thus the new society will spring into existence, ready equipped to perform all the useful functions of its predecessor.

• From *Socialism Made Easy*, a 1909 pamphlet. An earlier version of this text appeared as "Industrial Unionism" in *The Harp*, June 1908

What is the Sympathetic Strike?

What is the Sympathetic Strike? It is the recognition by the Working Class of their essential unity, the manifestation in our daily industrial relations that our brother's fight is our fight, our sister's troubles are our troubles, that we are all members one of another. In practical operation, it means that when any body of workers are in conflict with their employers, that all other workers should cooperate with them in attempting to bring that particular employer to reason by refusing to handle his goods. That in fact every employer who does not consent to treat his workpeople upon a civilised basis should be treated as an enemy of civilisation, and placed and kept outside the amenities and facilities offered by civilised communities.

In other words, that he and his should be made "tabu", treated as unclean, as "tainted", and therefore likely to contaminate all others. The idea is not new. It is as old as humanity. Several historical examples will readily occur to the mind of the thoughtful reader. The Vehmgerichte of Germany of the Middle Ages, where the offending person had a stake driven into the ground opposite his door by orders of the secret tribunal, and from that moment was as completely cut off from his fellows as if he were on a raft in mid-ocean, is one instance. The boycott of Land League days is another. In that boycott the very journals and politicians who are denouncing the Irish Transport Union used a weapon which in its actual operations was more merciless, cruel and repulsive than any Sympathetic Strike has ever yet been.

And even the Church, in its strength and struggles when it was able to command obedience to its decrees of excommunication, supplied history with a stern application of the same principle which, for thoroughness, we could never hope to equal.

Such instances could be almost indefinitely multiplied. When the peasants of France rose in the Jacquerie against their feudal barons, did not the English nobles join in sympathetic action with those French barons against the peasantry, although at that moment the English were in France as invaders and despoilers of the territory of those same French feudal barons? When the English peasantry revolted against their masters, did not all English aristocrats join in sympathetic action to crush them? When the German peasantry rose during the Reformation, did not Catholic and Protestant aristocrats cease exterminating each other to join in a sympathetic attempt to exterminate the insurgents? When, during the French Revolution, the French people overthrew kings and aristocrats, did not all the feudal lords and rulers of Europe take sympathetic action to restore the French monarchy, even although doing it involved throwing all industrial life in Europe into chaos and drenching a Continent with blood?

Historically, the sympathetic strike can find ample justification. But, and this point must be emphasised, it was not mere cool reasoning that gave it birth in Dublin. In this city it was born out of our desperate necessity. Seeing all classes of semi-skilled labour in Dublin so wretchedly underpaid and so atrociously sweated, the Irish Transport and General Workers' Union taught them to stand together and help one another, and out of this advice the more perfect weapon has grown. That the Labour movement here has utilised it before elsewhere is due to the fact that in this city what is known as general or unskilled labour bears a greater proportion to the whole body of workers than elsewhere. And hence the workers are a more moveable, fluctuating body, are more often as individuals engaged in totally dissimilar industries than in the English cities, where skilled trades absorb so great a proportion, and keep them so long in the one class of industry.

Out of all this turmoil and fighting the Union has evolved, is evolving, among its members a higher conception of mutual life, a realisation of their duties to each other and to society at large, and are thus building for the future in a way that ought to gladden the hearts of all lovers of the race. In contrast to the narrow, restricted outlook of the capitalist class, and even of certain old-fashioned trade-unionism, with their perpetual insistence upon "rights", this union insists, almost fiercely, that there are no rights without duties, and the first duty is to help one another. This is indeed revolutionary and disturbing, but not half as much as would be a practical following out of the moral precepts of Christianity.

For the immediate present, the way out of this deadlock is for all sides to consent to the formation of a Conciliation Board, before which all disputes must be brought. Let the employers insist upon levelling up the conditions of employment to one high standard; treat as an Ishmael any employer who refuses to conform, and leave him unassisted to fight the battle with the Union; let the Union proceed to organise all the workers possible, place all disputes as to wages before the Board for discussion, and only resort to a strike when agreement cannot be reached by the Board; and as all employers would be interested in bringing the more obdurate and greedy to reason, strikes would be rare. And when strikes were rare, the necessity for sympathetic strikes would also seldom develop.

Thus we will develop a social conscience, and lay the foundation for an orderly transformation of society in the future into a more perfect and a juster social order.

• Latter part of an article, "Labour in Dublin", in *The Irish Review*, October 1913

Police attack strikers on "Bloody Sunday", August 1913, Dublin

A Rebel Song

Come workers sing a rebel song,
A song of love and hate,
Of love unto the lowly
And of hatred to the great.
The great who trod our fathers down,
Who steal our children's bread,
Whose hands of greed are stretched to rob
The living and the dead.

[chorus:]

Then sing our rebel song as we proudly sweep along
To end the age-old tyranny that makes for human tears.
Our march is nearer done, with each setting of the sun.
And the tyrants' might is passing with the passing of the years.

We sing no more of wailing
And no songs of sighs or tears;
High are our hopes and stout our hearts
And banished all our fears.
Our flag is raised above us
So that all the world may see,
'Tis Labour's faith and Labour's arm
Alone can Labour free.

[chorus]

Out of the depths of misery
We march with hearts aflame;
With wrath against the rulers false
Who wreck our manhood's name.
The serf who licks the tyrant's rod
May bend forgiving knee;
The slave who breaks his slavery's chain
A wrathful man must be.

[chorus]

Our army marches onward
With its face towards the dawn,
In trust secure in that one thing
The slave may lean upon.
The might within the arm of him
Who knowing freedom's worth,
Strikes hard to banish tyranny
From off the face of earth.

— James Connolly, 1903

Industrialism and the Trade Unions

In the second part of my book *Socialism Made Easy*, I have endeavoured to establish two principles in the minds of my readers as being vitally necessary to the upbuilding of a strong revolutionary Socialist movement. Those two principles are: First, that the working class as a class cannot become permeated with a belief in the unity of their class interests unless they have first been trained to a realisation of the need of industrial unity; second, that the revolutionary act — the act of taking over the means of production and establishing a social order based upon the principles of the working class (labour) — cannot be achieved by a disorganised, defeated and humiliated working class, but must be the work of that class after it has attained to a commanding position on the field of economic struggle. It has been a pleasure to me to note the progress of Socialist thought towards acceptance of these principles, and to believe that the publication of that little work helped to a not inconsiderable degree in shaping that Socialist thought and in accelerating its progress. In the following article I wish to present one side of the discussion which inevitably arises in our Socialist party branches upon the mooting of this question.

But as a preliminary to this presentation I would like to decry, and ask my comrades to decry and dissociate themselves from, the somewhat acrid and intolerant manner in which this discussion is often carried on. Believing that the Socialist Party is part and parcel of the labour movement of the United States, and that in the growth of that movement to true revolutionary clearness and consciousness it, the Socialist Party, is bound to attract to itself and become mentor and teacher of elements most unclear and lacking in class consciousness, we should recognise that it is as much our duty to be patient and tolerant with the erring brother or sister within our ranks as with the rank heathen outside the fold. No good purpose can be served by wildly declaiming against "intellectuals", nor yet by intriguing against and misrepresenting "impossibilists". The comrades who think that the Socialist Party is run by "compromisers" should not jump out of the organisation and leave the revolutionists in a still more helpless minority; and the comrades who pride themselves upon being practical Socialist politicians should not too readily accuse those who differ with them of being potential disrupters.

Viewing the situation from the standpoint of an industrialist I am convinced that both the industrialist and those estimable comrades who pander to the old style trade unions to such a marked degree as to leave themselves open to the suspicion of coquetting with the idea of a "labour" party, both, I say, have the one belief, both have arrived at the one conclusion from such different angles that they appear as opposing instead of aiding, auxiliary forces. That belief which both share in common is that the triumph of Socialism is impossible without the aid of labour organised upon the economic field. It is their common possession of this one great principle of action which impels me to say that there is a greater identity of purpose and faith between those two opposing (?) wings of the Socialist Party than either can have with any of the intervening schools of thought. Both realise that the Socialist Party must rest upon the economic struggle and the forces of labour engaged therein, and that the Socialism which is not an outgrowth and expression of that economic struggle is not worth a moment's serious consideration.

There, then, we have found something upon which we agree, a ground common to both, the first desideratum of any serious discussion. The point upon which we disagree is: *Can the present form of American trade unions provide the Socialist movement with the economic force upon which to rest, or can the American Federation of Labour develop towards industrialism sufficiently for our needs?* It is the same problem stated in different ways. I propose to state here my reasons for taking the negative side in that discussion.

Let it be remembered that we are not, as some good comrades imagine, debating whether it is possible for a member of the American Federation of Labour to become an industrialist, or for all its members, but we are to debate whether the organisation of the American Federation of Labour is such as to permit of a modification of its structural formation to keep pace with the progress of industrialist ideas amongst its members. Whether the conversion of the membership of the American Federation of Labour to industrialism would mean the transformation of that body into an industrial organisation or the disruption of the Federation and the throwing of it aside as the up-to-date capitalist throws aside a machine, be it ever so costly, when a more perfectly functioning machine has been devised.

At this point it is necessary for the complete understanding of our subject that we step aside for a moment to consider the genesis and organisation of the American Federation of Labour and the trade unions patterned after it, and this involves a glance at the history of the labour movement in America. Perhaps of all the subjects properly pertaining to Socialist activity this subject has been the most neglected, the least analysed. And yet it is the most vital. Studies of Marx and popularising (sic) of Marx, studies of science and popularising of science, studies of religion and application of same with Socialist interpretations, all these we have without limit, but of attempts to apply the methods of Marx and of science to an analysis of the laws of growth and incidents of development of the organisations of labour upon the economic field the literature of the movement is almost, if not quite, absolutely barren. Our Socialist writers seem in some strange and, to me, incomprehensible manner to have detached themselves from the everyday struggles of the toilers and to imagine they are doing their whole duty as interpreters of Socialist thought when they bless the economic organisation with one corner of their mouth and insist upon the absolute hopelessness of it with the other. They imagine, of course, that this is the astutest diplomacy, but the net result of it has been that the organised working class has never looked upon the Socialist Party as a part of the labour movement, and the enrolled Socialist Party member has never found in American Socialist literature anything that helped him in strengthening his economic organisation or leading it to victory.

Perhaps some day there will arise in America a Socialist writer who in his writing will live up to the spirit of the Communist Manifesto that the Socialists are not apart from the labour movement, are not a sect, but are simply that part of the working class which pushes on all others, which most clearly understands the line of march.

Awaiting the advent of that writer permit me to remind our readers that the Knights of Labour preceded the American Federation of Labour, that the structural formation of the Knights was that of a mass organisation, that they aimed to organise all toilers into one union and made no distinction of craft, *nor of industry*, and that they cherished revolutionary aims. When the American Federation of Labour was organised it was organised as a dual organisation, and although at first it professed a desire to organise none but those then unorganised, it soon developed opposition to the Knights and proceeded to organise wherever it could find members, and particularly to seek after the enrolment of those who were already in the Knights of Labour. In this it was assisted by the good will of the master class, who naturally preferred its profession of conservatism and identity of interest between capital and labour to the revolutionary aims and methods of the Knights. But even this assistance on the part of the master class would not have assured its victory were it not for the fact that its method of organisation, *into separate crafts*, recognised a certain need of the industrial development of the time which the Knights of Labour had failed up to that moment to appraise at its proper significance.

The Knights of Labour, as I have pointed out, organised all workers into one union, an excellent idea for teaching the toilers their ultimate class interests, but with the defect that it made no provision for the treating of special immediate craft interests by men and women with the requisite technical knowledge.

The scheme was the scheme of an idealist, too large-hearted and noble-minded himself to appreciate the hold small interests can have upon men and women. It gave rise to jealousies. The printer grumbled at the jurisdiction of a body comprising tailors and shoemakers over his shop struggles, and the tailors and shoemakers fretted at the attempts of carpenters and bricklayers to understand the technicalities of their disputes with the bosses.

To save the Knights of Labour and to save the American working class a pilgrimage in the desert of reaction, it but required the advent of some practical student of industry to propose that, instead of massing all workers together irrespective of occupation, they should, keeping the organisation intact and remaining bound in obedience to one supreme head, *for administrative purposes only*, group all workers together according to their industries, and subdivide their industries again according to crafts. That the allied crafts should select the ruling body for the industry to which they belonged, and that the allied industries again should elect the ruling body for the whole organisation. This could have been done without the slightest jar to the framework of the organisation; it would have recognised all technical differences and specialisation of function in actual industry; it would have kept the organisation of labour in line with the actual progress of industrial development; and would still have kept intact the idea of the unity of the working class by its common bond of brotherhood, a universal membership card, and universal obligation to recognise that an injury to one was an injury to all.

Tentative steps in such a direction were already being taken when the American Federation of Labour came upon the scene. The promoters of this organisation, seizing upon this one plank in the Knights of Labour organisation, specialised its work along that line, and, instead of hastening to save the unity of the working class on the lines above indicated, they made the growing realisation of the need of representation of craft differences the entering wedge for disrupting and destroying the earlier organisation of that class.

Each craft was organised as a distinct body having no obligation to strike or fight beside any other craft, and making its own contracts with the bosses heedless of what was happening between these bosses and their fellow-labourers of another craft in the same industry, building, shop or room. The craft was organised on a national basis, to be governed by the vote of its members throughout the nation, and with a membership card good only in that craft and of no use to a member who desired to leave one craft in order to follow another. The fiction of national unity was and is still paid homage to, as vice always pays homage to virtue, by annual congresses in which many resolutions are gravely debated, to be forgotten as soon as congress adjourns. But the unifying (?) qualities of this form of organisation are best revealed by the fact that the main function of the congress seems to be to provide the cynical master class with the, to them, pleasing spectacle of allied organisations fiercely fighting over questions of jurisdiction.

This policy of the American Federation of Labour coupled with the unfortunate bomb incident of Chicago, for which the Knights of Labour received much of the blame, completed the ruin of the latter organisation and destroyed the growing unity of the working class for the time being. The industrial union, as typified today in the Industrial Workers of the World, could have, as I have shown, developed out of the Knights of Labour as logically and perfectly as the adult develops from the child. No new organisation would have been necessary, and hence we may conclude that the Industrial Workers of the World is the legitimate heir of the native American labour movement, the inheritor of its principles, and the ripened fruit of its experiences. On the other hand the American Federation of Labour may truly be regarded as a usurper on the throne of labour, a usurper who occupies the throne by virtue of having strangled its predecessor, and now, like all usurpers, raises the cry of "treason" against the rightful heir when it seeks to win its own again. It is obvious that the sway of the American Federation of Labour in the American labour movement is but a brief interregnum between the passing of the old revolutionary organisation and the ascension into power of the new.

But, I fancy I hear some one say, granting that all that is true, may we not condemn the methods by which the American Federation of Labour destroyed, or helped to destroy, the Knights of Labour, and still believe that out of the American Federation of Labour we may now build up an industrial organisation such as we need, such as the Industrial Workers of the World aims to be?

This we can only answer by clearly focusing in our mind the American Federation of Labour system of organisation in actual practice. A carpenter is at work in a city. He has a dispute with the bosses, or all his fellow-carpenters have. They will hold meetings to discuss the question of a strike, and finding the problem too big for them they will pass it on to the headquarters, and the headquarters pass it on to the general membership. The general membership, from San Francisco to Rhode Island, and from Podunk to Kalamazoo, will have a vote and say upon the question of the terms upon which the Chicago carpenters work, and if said carpenters are called out they will expect all these widely scattered carpenters to support them by financial and moral help. But while they are soliciting and receiving the support of their fellow-carpenters from Dan to Beeshebee they are precluded from calling out in sympathy with them the painters who follow them in their work, the plumbers whose pipes they cover up, the steamfitters who work at their elbows, or the plasterer who precedes them. Yet the co-operation of these workers with them in their strikes is a thousandfold more important than the voting of strike funds which would keep them out on strike — until the building season is over and the winter sets in. In many cities today there is a Building Trades Council which is looked upon by many as a beginning of industrialism within the American Federation of Labour. It is not only the beginning but it is as far as industrialism can go within that body, and its sole function is to secure united action in remedying petty grievances and enforcing the observance of contracts, but it does not take part in the really important work of determining hours or wages. It cannot for the simple reason that each of the thirty-three unions in the building industry are international organisations with international officers, and necessitating international referendums before any strikes, looking to the fixing of hours or wages, are permissible. Hence, although all the building trade branches in a given district may be satisfied that the time is ripe for obtaining better conditions, they cannot act before they obtain the consent of the membership throughout the entire country, and before that is obtained the moment for action is passed. The bond that is supposed to unite the carpenter in New York with the carpenter in Kokomo, Indiana, is converted into a wall of isolation which prevents him uniting, except in the most perfunctory fashion, with the men of other crafts who work beside him. The industrial union and the craft union are mutually exclusive terms. Suppose all the building trades branches of Chicago resolved to unite industrially to form an industrial union. Every branch which became an integral part of said union, pledged to obey its call to action, would by so doing forfeit its charter in the craft union and in the American Federation of Labour, and outside Chicago its members would be considered as scabs.

The Brewers Union has been fighting for years to obtain the right to organise all brewery employees. It is hindered from doing so, not only by the rules of the American Federation of Labour, but by the form of organisation of that body. Breweries, for instance, employ plumbers. Now if a plumber, so employed, would join the Brewers Union and obey its call to strike he would be expelled from his craft union, and if he ever lost his job in the brewery would be considered as a scab if he went to work where union plumbers were employed. A craft union cannot recognise the right of another association to call its members out on a strike. A machinist works today in a machine shop; a few months from now he may be employed in a clothing factory attending to the repairs of sewing machines. If the clothing industry resolves itself into an industrial union and he joins them, as he needs must if he believes in industrialism, he loses his membership in the International Association of Machinists, and if ever he loses his factory job and seeks to return to the machine shop he must either do so as a non-union man or pay a heavy fine if he is permitted to re-enter the

International Association of Machinists. A stationary engineer works today at the construction of a new building, three months from now he is in a shipyard, six months from now he is at the mouth of a coal mine. Three different industries, requiring three different industrial unions.

The craft card is good today in all of them, but if any of them chose to form industrial unions, and called upon him to join, he could only do so on penalty of losing his craft card and his right to strike benefits from his old organisation. And if he did join, his card of membership in the one he joined would be of no value when he drifted to any of the others. How can the American Federation of Labour avoid this dilemma? Industrialism requires that all the workers in a given industry be subject to the call of the governing body, or of the vote of the workers in that industry. But if these workers are organised in the American Federation of Labour they must be subject only to the call of their national or international craft body; and if at any time they obey the call of the industry in preference to the craft they are ordered peremptorily back to scab upon their brothers.

If in addition to this organic difficulty, and it is the most insuperable, we take into consideration the system of making contracts or trade agreements on a craft basis pursued by old style unions we will see that our unfortunate brothers in the American Federation of Labour are tied hand and foot, handcuffed and hobbled, to prevent their advance into industrialism. During the recent shirt-waist makers' strike in New York when the question was mooted of a similar strike in Philadelphia our comrade Rose Pastor Stokes, according to our Socialist press, was continually urging upon the shirt-waist makers of Philadelphia the wisdom of striking before Christmas, and during the busy season. No more sensible advice could have been given. It was of the very essence of industrialist philosophy. Industrialism is more than a method of organisation — it is a science of fighting. It says to the worker: fight only at the time you select, never when the boss wants a fight. Fight at the height of the busy season, and in the slack season when the workers are in thousands upon the sidewalk absolutely refuse to be drawn into battle. Even if the boss insults and vilifies your union and refuses to recognise it, take it lying down in the slack season but mark it up in your little note book. And when work is again rushing and Master Capitalist is pressed for orders squeeze him, and squeeze him till the most sensitive portion of his anatomy, his pocket-book, yells with pain. That is the industrialist idea of the present phase of the class war as organised labour should conduct it. But, whatever may have been the case with the shirt-waist makers, that policy so ably enunciated by comrade Rose Pastor Stokes is utterly opposed to the whole philosophy and practice of the American Federation of Labour. Contracts almost always expire when there is little demand for labour.

For instance the United Mine Workers' contract with the bosses expires in the early summer when they have before them a long hot season with a minimum demand for coal. Hence the expiration of the contract generally finds the coal operators spoiling for a fight, and the union secretly dreading it. Most building trade contracts with the bosses expire in the winter. For example, the Brotherhood of Carpenters in New York, their contract expires in January. A nice time for a fight, in the middle of a northern winter, when all work in their vicinity is suspended owing to the rigours of the climate!

The foregoing will, I hope, give the reader some food for consideration upon the problem under review. That problem is intimately allied with the future of the Socialist Party in America. Our party must become the political expression of the fight in the workshop, and draw its inspiration therefrom. Everything which tends to strengthen and discipline the hosts of labour tends irresistibly to swell the ranks of the revolutionary movement, and everything which tends to divide and disorganise the hosts of labour tends also to strengthen the forces of capitalism. *The most dispersive and isolating force at work in the labour movement today is craft unionism, the most cohesive and unifying force, industrial unionism.* In view of that fact all objections which my comrades make to industrial unionism on the grounds of the supposedly, or truly, anti-political bias of many members of the Industrial Workers of the World is quite beside the mark. That question at the present stage of the game is purely doctrinaire. The use or non-use of political action will not be settled by the doctrinaires who may make it their hobby today, but will be settled by the workers who use the Industrial Workers of the World in their workshop struggles. And if at any time the conditions of a struggle in shop, factory, railroad or mine necessitate the employment of political action those workers so organised will use it, all theories and theorists to the contrary notwithstanding.

In their march to freedom the workers will use every weapon they find necessary.

As the economic struggle is the preparatory school and training ground for Socialists it is our duty to help guide along right lines the effort of the workers to choose the correct kind of organisation to fight their battles in that conflict. According as they choose aright or wrongly, so will the development of class consciousness in their minds be hastened or retarded by their everyday experience in class struggles.

• *International Socialist Review*, February 1910

Industrial and Political Unity

"The great strike of the shop employees on the Canadian Pacific Railway has been declared off — lost. While the shopmen were fighting desperately to maintain their organisation and decent working conditions, the engineers, firemen, conductors, trainmen, etc., worked with scabs imported from the states and from Europe, and thus by keeping trains moving aided to break the strike. It is only one more illustration of what a vicious, not to say downright criminal, scheme craft autonomy actually is in practice.

"Here's another example: After four years of hard fighting from the Mississippi river to the Pacific coast and from the Ohio river to the Gulf, the machinists have been compelled to abandon their strikes on the Santa Fe and the L. & N. railways. The engines and cars built and repaired in the railway shops by strike-breakers were hauled over the roads by members of the old brotherhoods without the slightest objections, No wonder that onlookers become disgusted with such 'unionism'. Some union cards cover a multitude of sins."

— *Max Hayes in* International Socialist Review

At meetings throughout this country one frequently hears speakers labouring to arouse the workers to their duty, exclaiming:

"You unite industrially, why then do you divide politically? You unite against the bosses in strikes and lock-outs, and then you foolishly divide when you go to the ballot-box. Why not unite at the ballot-box as you unite in the workshop? Why not show the same unity on the political field as you do on the industrial battlefield?"

At first blush this looks to be an exceedingly apt and forcible form of appeal to our fellow-workers, but when examined more attentively it will be seen that in view of the facts of our industrial warfare this appeal is based upon a flagrant mis-statement of facts. The real truth is that the workers do not unite industrially, but on the contrary are most hopelessly divided on the industrial field, and that their division and confusion on the political field are the direct result of their division and confusion on the industrial field. It would be easy to prove that even our most loyal trade unionists habitually play the game of the capitalist class on the industrial field just as surely as the Republican and Democratic workers do it on the political field. Let us examine the situation on the industrial field and see if it justifies the claim that economically the workers are united, or if it justifies the contention we make that the division of the workers on the political field is but the reflex of the confused ideas derived from the practice of the workers in strikes and lock-outs.

Quite recently we had a great strike of the workers employed on the Subway and Elevated systems of street car service in New York. The men showed a splendid front against the power of the mammoth capitalist company headed by August Belmont, against which they were arrayed. Conductors, motormen, ticket-choppers, platform men, repairers, permanent way men, ticket-sellers — all went out together and for a time paralysed the entire traffic on their respective system. The company, on the other hand, had the usual recourse to Jim Farley and his scabs and sought to man the trains with those professional traitors to their class. The number of scabs was large, but small in proportion to the men on strike, yet the strike was broken. It was not the scabs, however, who turned the scale against the strikers in favour of the men. That service to capital was performed by good union men with union cards in their pockets. These men were the engineers in the power houses which supplied the electric power to run the cars, and without whom all the scabs combined could not have run a single trip. A scab is a vile creature, but what shall we say of the men who helped the scab to commit his act of treason. The law says that an accessory before the fact is equally guilty of a crime with the actual criminal. What, then, are the trade unionists who supplied the power to scabs to help them to break a strike? They were unconsciously being compelled by their false system of organisation to betray their struggling brothers. Was this unity on the industrial field? And is it any wonder that the men accustomed to so scab upon their fellow-workers in a labour struggle should also scab it upon their class in a political struggle? Is it not rather common sense to expect that the recognition of the necessity for concerted common action of all workers against the capitalist enemy in the industrial battle ground must precede the realisation of the wisdom of common action as a class on the political battlefield? The men who are taught that it is all right to continue working for a capitalist against whom their shop-mates of a different craft are on strike are not likely to see any harm in continuing to vote for a capitalist nominee at the polls even when he is opposed by a candidate of a Socialist and labour organisation. Political scabbery is born of industrial scabbery; it is its legitimate offspring.

Instances of this industrial disunion could be cited indefinitely. The Longshoremen of the Port of New York went out on strike. They at first succeeded in tying up the ships of the Shipping Trust, great as its wealth is, and in demonstrating the real power of labour when unhampered by contracts with capital.

The Shipping Trust was taken by surprise, but quickly recovered, and as usual imported scabs from all over the country. Then was seen what the unity of the working class on the industrial field amounts to under present conditions. As scab longshoremen unloaded the ship, union teamsters with union buttons in their hats received the goods from their hands, loaded them into their teams, and drove merrily away.

As scab longshoremen loaded a ship union men coaled it, and when the cargo was safely on board union marine engineers set up steam, and union seamen and firemen took it out of the dock on its voyage to its destination. Can men who are trained and taught to believe that such a course of conduct is right and proper be expected to realise the oneness of the interests of the working class as a whole against the capitalist class as a whole, and vote and act accordingly? In short, can their field of vision be so extensive that it can see the brotherhood of all men, and yet so restricted that it can see no harm in a brother labour organisation in the one industry being beaten to death by capital?

Contrast this woeful picture of divided and disorganised "unionism" in America with the following account from the *New York Sun* of the manner in which the Socialist unionists of Scandinavia stand together in a fight against the common enemy, irrespective of "craft interests" or "craft contracts":

> *"A short sojourn in Scandinavia, particularly in Copenhagen and the southern part of Sweden, gives one an object lesson in socialism. In some way or other the socialists have managed to capture all the trade unions in these parts and between them have caused a regime of terror for everybody who is unfortunate enough to own a business of any sort. Heaven help him if he fires one of his help or tries to assert himself in any way. He is immediately declared in 'blockade'.*
>
> *"This socialistic term means practically the same as a boycott. If the offending business man happens to be a retail merchant all workmen are warned off his premises. The drivers for the wholesale houses refuse to deliver goods at his store; the truck-men refuse to cart anything to or from his place, and so on; in fact, he is a doomed man unless he comes to terms with the union. It is worth mentioning that boycotting bulletins and also the names and addresses of those who are bold enough to help the man out are published in leaded type in all the socialistic newspapers. A law to prevent the publication of such boycotting announcements was proposed in the Swedish Riksdag this year, but was defeated.*
>
> *"If the boycotted person be a wholesale dealer the proceedings are much the same or, rather, they are reversed. The retailers are threatened with the loss of the workmen's trade unless they cease dealing with such a firm; the truck-*

men refuse to haul for it. It has even happened that the scavengers have refused to remove the refuse from the premises. More often, however, the cans are 'accidentally' dropped on the stairs. These scavengers belong to the cities' own forces, as a rule, and receive pensions after a certain length of service, but they have all sworn allegiance to the socialistic cause.

"In reading the foregoing it is well to remember that practically all the workingmen of such cities — that is, practically all Sweden and Denmark — are union men, i. e., socialists, and are therefore able to carry out their threats".

Here we have a practical illustration of the power of Socialism when it rests upon an economic organisation, and the effectiveness and far-reaching activity of unionism when it is inspired by the Socialist ideal. Now as an equally valuable object lesson in American unionism, an object lesson in how not to do it, let us picture a typical state of affairs in the machine industry. The moulders' contract with the boss expires and they go out on strike. In a machine shop the moulder occupies a position intermediate between the patternmaker and the machinist, or, as they are called in Ireland, the engineers. When the moulders go out the boss who has had all his plans laid for months beforehand brings in a staff of scabs and installs them in the places of the striking workers. Then the tragicomedy begins. The union patternmaker makes his patterns and hands them over to the scab moulder; the scab moulder casts his moulds and when they are done the union machinist takes them from him and placidly finishes the job. Then having finished their day's work, they go to their union meetings and vote donations of a few hundred dollars to help the strikers to defeat the boss, after they had worked all day to help the boss to defeat the strikers. Thus they exemplify the solidarity of labour. When the moulders are beaten the machinists and the patternmakers, and the blacksmiths, and the electricians, and the engineers, and all the rest take their turn of going up against the boss in separate bodies to be licked. As each is taking its medicine its fellows of other crafts in the same shop sympathise with it in the name of the solidarity of labour, and continue to work in the service of the capitalist, against whom the strike is directed, in the name of the sacred contract of the craft union.

When the coal miners of Pennsylvania had their famous strike in 1902 the railroad brotherhoods hauled in scabs to take their places, and when the scabs had mined coal the same railroad men hauled out this scab-mined coal.

Need we go on to prove our point that industrial division and discord is the order of the day amongst the workers, and that this disunion and confusion on the economic field cannot fail to perpetuate itself upon the political field. Those orators who reproach the workers with being divided on the political field, although united on the industrial, are simply misstating facts. The workers are divided on both, and as political parties are the reflex of economic conditions, it follows that industrial union once established will create the political unity of the working class. We feel that we cannot too strongly insist upon this point. Political division is born of industrial division; political scabbery is born of industrial craft scabbery; political weakness keeps even step with industrial weakness. It is an axiom enforced by all the experience of the ages that they who rule industrially will rule politically, and therefore they who are divided and wrongly organised industrially will remain impotent politically. The failure of Mr. Gompers to unite politically the force of the American Federation of Labour was the inevitable outcome of his own policy of division on the industrial battle ground; he reversed the natural process by trying to unite men on class lines whilst he opposed every effort, as in the case of the Brewers, to unite them on industrial lines. The natural lines of thought and action lead from the direct to the indirect, from the simple to the complex, from the immediate to the ultimate. Mr. Gompers ignored this natural line of development and preached the separation into craft organisations, with separate craft interests of the workers, and then expected them to heed his call to unity on the less direct and immediate battleground of politics. He failed, as even the Socialists would fail if they remained equally blind to the natural law of our evolution into class consciousness. That natural law leads us as individuals to unite in our craft, as crafts to unite in our industry, as industries in our class, and the finished expression of that evolution is, we believe, the appearance of our class upon the political battle-ground with all the economic power behind it to enforce its mandates. Before that day dawns our political parties of the working class are but propagandist agencies, John the Baptists of the New Redemption, but when that day dawns our political party will be armed with all the might of our class; will be revolutionary in fact as well as in thought.

To Irish men and women especially we do not need, we feel, to labour this point. The historic example of the Land League bequeaths to us a precious legacy of wisdom, both practical and revolutionary, shaping our course of action. During Land League days in Ireland when a tenant was evicted from a farm, not only his fellow-tenants but practically the whole country united to help him in his fight. When the evicted farm was rented by another tenant, a land-grabber or "scab", every person in the countryside shunned him as a leper, and, still better, fought him as a traitor. Nor did they make the mistake of fighting the traitor and yet working for his employer, the landlord. No, they included both in the one common hostility.

At the command of the Land League every servant and labourer quit the service of the landlord. In Ireland, it is well to remember, in order to appreciate this act of the labourers, that the landlords were usually better paymasters and more generous employers than the tenant farmers. The labourers, therefore, might reasonably have argued that the fight of the tenant farmers was none of their business. But they indulged in no such blindly selfish hair-splitting. When the landlord had declared war upon the tenant by evicting him, the labourers responded by war upon the landlord. Servant boy and servant girl at once quit his service, the carman refused to drive him, the cook to cook for him, his linen remained unwashed, his harvest unreaped, his cows unmilked, his house and fields deserted. The grocer and the butcher, the physician and the schoolmaster were alike hostile to him; if the children of the land-grabber (scab) entered school all other children rose and left; if the land-grabber or his landlord attended Mass everyone else at Mass walked out in a body. They found it hard to get anyone to serve them or feed them in health, to attend them in sickness, or to bury those dear to them in death. It was this relentless and implacable war upon the landowning class and traitors among the tenant class which gave the word "boycott" to the English language through its enforcement against an Irish landowner, Captain Boycott. It was often horrible, it was always ugly in appearance to the superficial observer, but it was marvellously effective. It put courage and hope and manhood into a class long reckoned as the most enslaved in Europe. It broke the back of the personal despotism of the Irish landlord and so crippled his social and economic power that Irish landed estates from being a favourite form of investment for the financial interests sank to such a position that even the most reckless moneylender would for a time scarce accept a mortgage upon them. That it failed of attaining real economic freedom for the Irish people was due not to any defect in its method of fighting, but rather to the fact that economic questions are not susceptible of being settled within the restricted radius of any one small nation, but are acted upon by influences world-wide in their character.

But how great a lesson for the American worker is to be found in this record of a class struggle in Ireland! The American worker was never yet so low in the social and political scale as the Irish tenant. Yet the Irish tenant rose and by sheer force of his unity on the economic field shattered the power of his master, whilst the American worker remaining divided upon the economic field sinks day by day lower toward serfdom. The Irish tenant had to contend against the overwhelming power of a foreign empire backing up the economic power of a native tyranny, yet he conquered, whilst the American worker able to become the political sovereign of the country remains the sport of the political factions of his masters and the slave of their social power.

The Irish tenant uniting on the economic field felt his strength, and, carrying the fight into politics, simply swept into oblivion every individual or party that refused to serve his class interests, but the American toilers remain divided on the economic field, and hence are divided and impotent upon the political, zealous servants of every interest but their own.

Need we point the moral more. Every one who has the interests of the working class at heart, every one who wishes to see the Socialist Party command the allegiance of the political hosts of labour, should strive to realise industrial union as the solid foundation upon which alone the political unity of the workers can be built up and directed toward a revolutionary end. To this end all those who work for industrial unionism are truly co-operating even when they least care for political activities.

• *The Harp*, December 1908

Cartoon by Ernest Kavanagh in the Irish Worker, in 1913, following August's police brutality. The figure on the right is Lorcan G. Sherlock, the Irish Nationalist Party Mayor of Dublin, white-washing this police brutality.

The Irish Citizen Army outside Liberty Hall, Dublin, 1914, under a banner which reads "We Serve Neither King Nor Kaiser, But Ireland!"

The ICA was a small paramilitary group of trained trade union volunteers from the Irish Transport and General Workers' Union (ITGWU) established in Dublin for the defence of workers' demonstrations from the Dublin Metropolitan Police. It was formed by Jim Larkin, James Connolly and Jack White on 23 November 1913.

Liberty Hall was, as seen in the picture, the head office of the ITGWU.

The Dublin Lockout: On the Eve

Perhaps before this issue of *The Irish Worker* is in the hands of its readers the issues now at stake in Dublin will be brought to a final determination. All the capitalist newspapers of Friday last join in urging, or giving favourable publicity to the views of others urging the employers of Dublin to join in a general lock-out of the members of the Irish Transport and General Workers' Union. It is as well. Possibly some such act is necessary in order to make that portion of the working class which still halts undecided to understand clearly what it is that lies behind the tyrannical and brow-beating attitude of the proprietors of the Dublin tramway system.

The fault of the Transport Union! What is it? Let us tell it in plain language. Its fault is this, that it found the labourers of Ireland on their knees, and has striven to raise them to the erect position of manhood; it found them with all the vices of slavery in their souls, and it strove to eradicate these vices and replace them with some of the virtues of free men; it found them with no other weapons of defence than the arts of the liar, the lickspittle, and the toady, and it combined them and taught them to abhor those arts and rely proudly on the defensive power of combination; it, in short, found a class in whom seven centuries of social outlawry had added fresh degradations upon the burden it bore as the members of a nation suffering from the cumulative effects of seven centuries of national bondage, and out of this class, the degraded slaves of slaves more degraded still — for what degradation is more abysmal than that of those who prostitute their manhood on the altar of profit-mongering? — out of this class of slaves the labourers of Dublin, the Transport Union has created an army of intelligent self-reliant men, abhorring the old arts of the toady, the lickspittle, and the crawler and trusting alone to the disciplined use of their power to labour or to withdraw their labour to assert and maintain their right as men.

To put it in other words, but words as pregnant with truth and meaning: the Irish Transport Workers' Union found that before its advent the working class of Dublin had been taught by all the educational agencies of the country, by all the social influences of their masters, that this world was created for the special benefit of the various sections of the master class, that kings and lords and capitalists were of value; that even flunkeys, toadies, lickspittle and poodle dogs had an honoured place in the scheme of the universe, but that there was neither honour, credit, nor consideration to the man or woman who toils to maintain them all. Against all this the Transport Union has taught that they who toil are the only ones that do matter, that all others are but beggars upon the bounty of those who work with hand or brain, and that this superiority of social value can at any time be realised, be translated into actual fact, by the combination of the labouring class. Preaching, organising, and fighting upon this basis, the Transport Union has done what? If the value of a city is to be found in the development of self-respect and high conception of social responsibilities among a people, then the Irish Transport Union found Dublin the poorest city in these countries by reason of its lack of these qualities.

And by imbuing the workers with them, it has made Dublin the richest city in Europe today, rich by all that counts for greatness in the history of nations. It is then upon this working class so enslaved, this working class so led and so enriched with moral purposes and high aims, that the employers propose to make general war.

Shall we shrink from it; cower before their onset? A thousand times no! Shall we crawl back into our slums, abase our hearts, bow our knees, and crawl once more to lick the hand that would smite us? Shall we, who have been carving out for our children a brighter future, a cleaner city, a freer life, consent to betray them instead into the grasp of the blood-suckers from whom we have dreamt of escaping? No, no, and yet again no. Let them declare their lock-out; it will only hasten the day when the working class will lock-out the capitalist class for good and all. If for taking the side of the Tram men we are threatened with suffering, why we have suffered before. But let them understand well that once they start that ball rolling no capitalist power on earth can prevent it continuing to roll, that every day will add to the impetus it will give to the working class purpose, to the thousands it will bring to the working class ranks and every added suffering inflicted upon the workers will be a fresh obstacle in the way of moderation when the day of final settlement arrives.

Yes, indeed, if it is going to be a wedding, let it be a wedding; and if it is going to be a wake, let it be a wake: *we are ready for either.*

• *The Irish Worker*, 30 August 1913. There titled: "If it is going to be a wedding, let it be a wedding; and if it is going to be a wake, let it be a wake".

Glorious Dublin!

To the readers of *Forward* possibly some sort of apology is due for the non-appearance of my notes for the past few weeks, but I am sure that they quite well understand that I was, so to speak, otherwise engaged. On the day I generally write my little screed, I was engaged on the 31st of August in learning how to walk around in a ring with about 40 other unfortunates kept six paces apart, and yet slip in a word or two to the poor devil in front of or behind me without being noticed by the watchful prison warders.

The first question I asked was generally "say, what are you in for?" Then the rest of the conversation ran thus:

"For throwing stones at the police."

"Well, I hope you did throw them and hit."

"No, by God, that's the worst of it. I was pulled coming out of my own house."

"Pulled" is the Dublin word for arrested. It was somewhat mortifying to me to know that I was the only person apparently in prison who had really committed the crime for which I was arrested. It gave me a sort of feeling that I was lowering the moral tone of the prison by coming amongst such a crowd of blameless citizens.

But the concluding part of our colloquy was a little more encouraging. It usually finished in this way:

"Are you in the Transport Union?"

"Of course I am."

"Good. Well if they filled all the prisons in Ireland they can't beat us, my boy."

"No, thank God, they can't; we'll fight all the better when we get out."

And there you have the true spirit. Baton charges, prison cells, untimely death and acute starvation — all were faced without a murmur, and in face of them all, the brave Dublin workers never lost faith in their ultimate triumph, never doubted but that their organisation would emerge victorious from the struggle. This is the great fact that many of our critics amongst the English Labour leaders seem to lose sight of. The Dublin fight is more than a trade union fight; it is a great class struggle, and recognised as such by all sides. We in Ireland feel that to doubt our victory would be to lose faith in the destiny of our class.

I heard of one case where a labourer was asked to sign the agreement forswearing the Irish Transport and General Workers' Union, and he told his employer, a small capitalist builder, that he refused to sign. The employer, knowing the man's circumstances, reminded him that he had a wife and six children who would be starving within a week. The reply of this humble labourer rose to the heights of sublimity. "It is true, sir," he said, "they will starve; but I would rather see them go out one by one in their coffins than that I should disgrace them by signing that."

And with head erect he walked out to share hunger and privation with his loved ones. Hunger and privation — and honour.

Defeat, bah! How can such a people be defeated? His case is typical of thousands more. Take the case of the United Builders Labourers' Trade Union, for instance. This was a rival union to the Irish Transport and General Workers' Union. Many sharp passages had occurred between them, and the employers counted confidently upon their cooperation in the struggle; Mr. William Martin Murphy especially praising them and exulting in their supposed acquiescence in his plans.

Remember also that they were a dividing society, dividing their funds at the end of each year, and therefore without any strike funds. When the members of their union were asked to sign the agreement, promising never to join or help the Transport Union, not one man consented — but all over Dublin their 2,500 members marched out "to help the Transport boys." Long ere these lines are written, they have experienced all the horrors of starvation, but with grim resolve they have tightened their belts and presented an unyielding front to the enemy.

It is a pleasure to me to recall that I was a member of their Union before I went to America, and that they twice ran me as their candidate for Dublin City Council before the Irish Transport and General Workers' Union was dreamed of, or before our friend Jim Larkin brought the aid of his wonderful magnetism to the Labour movement in Ireland.

What is true of that union is also true of most of the skilled trades. All are showing wonderful loyalty to their class. Coachbuilders, sawyers, engineers, bricklayers, each trade that is served by general labourers, walks out along with the Transport boys; refuses to even promise to work with any one who signs the employers' agreement, and, cheering, lines up along with their class.

Or think of the heroic women and girls. Did they care to evade the issue, they might have remained at work, for the first part of the agreement asks them to merely repudiate the Transport Workers, and as women they are members of the Irish Women Workers' Union, not of the Transport. But the second part pledges them to refuse to "help" the Transport Union — and in every shop, factory and sweating hell-hole in Dublin, as the agreement is presented, they march out with pinched faces, threadbare clothes, and miserable footgear, but with high hopes, undaunted spirit, and glorious resolve shining out of their eyes. Happy the men who will secure such wives; thrice blessed the nation which has such girls as the future mothers of the race!

Ah, comrades, it is good to have lived in Dublin in these days!

And then our friends write deprecatingly to the British press of the "dislocation of trade" involved in sympathetic strikes, of the "perpetual conflicts" in which they would involve great trade unions. To those arguments, if we can call them such, our answer is sufficient. It is this:

If the capitalist class knew that any outrages upon a worker, any attack upon labour, would result in a prompt dislocation of trade, perhaps national in its extent; that the unions were prepared to spend their last copper if necessary rather than permit a brother or sister to be injured, then the knowledge would not only ensure a long cessation from industrial skirmishing such as the unions are harassed by today, it would not only ensure peace to the unions, but what is of vastly more importance, it would ensure to the individual worker a peace from slave-driving and harassing at his work such as the largest unions are apparently unable to guarantee under present methods.

Mark, when I say "prepared to spend their last copper if necessary," I am not employing merely a rhetorical flourish, I am using the words literally. As we believe that in the Socialist Society of the future the entire resources of the nation must stand behind every individual, guaranteeing him against want, so today our unions must be prepared to fight with all their resources to safeguard the rights of every individual member.

The adoption of such a principle, followed by a few years of fighting on such lines to convince the world of our earnestness, would not only transform the industrial arena, but would revolutionise politics. Each side would necessarily seek to grasp the power of the state to reinforce its position, and politics would thus become what they ought to be, a reflex of the industrial battle, and lose the power to masquerade as a neutral power detached from economic passions or motives.

At present I regret to say Labour politicians seem to be losing all reality as effective aids to our struggles on the industrial battlefield, are becoming more and more absorbed in questions of administration, or taxation, and only occasionally, as in the Miners' National Strike, really rise to a realisation of their true role of Parliamentary outposts of the industrial army.

The Parliamentary tail in Britain still persist in wagging the British industrial dog. Once the dog really begins to assert his true position, we will be troubled no more by carping critics of labour politics, nor yet with Labour politicians' confessions of their own impotence in such great crises as that of the railway strike or the Johannesburg massacres.

Nor yet would we see that awful spectacle we have seen lately of labour politicians writing to the capitalist press to denounce the methods of a union which, with 20,000 men and women locked out in one city, is facing an attempt of 400 employers to starve its members back into slavery.

And thou, Brutus, that you should play the enemy's game at such a crisis! Every drop of ink you spilled in such an act stopped a loaf of bread on its way to some starving family [...]

The following letter appeared in the Dublin *Irish Times* and is a gem that the readers of *Forward* should appreciate:

The Labour Crisis in Dublin: Sir — Proverbially akin, tragedy and comedy have apparently joined in their final embrace. Released last week from Mountjoy Jail for the same offence, the allied protagonists of Liberty Hall — James Larkin and James Connolly — have upset many important institutions and queered not a few pitches!

Yesterday, at the same moment, while the Rev. Father Condon, O.S.A., uttered the thunders of Rome to "the Grand Annual Office of the United Confraternities of Dublin in honour of the Blessed Virgin" against Larkin and his works, James Connolly was received in the streets of Belfast with volleys of stones, accompanied with cries of "No Pope!"

What under Heaven does it all really mean?

Who said a "sympathetic strike?"

Yours, etc. — A Disciple of the late W S Gilbert. Dublin, 18th September, 1913.

• *Forward*, 4 October 1913. The pluristop [...] near the end indicates that in his *Forward* article Connolly reproduced a section from his text on "What is the Sympathetic Strike?" included in this booklet.

The Isolation of Dublin

I want this week to talk about the "isolation of Dublin". Some seven or eight weeks ago the proposal to isolate Dublin was the subject of much controversy in the Labour papers, and much fierce comment in the capitalist press. It is my desire in this week's article to tell how and in what manner the proposal was carried through, and how it is that now Dublin is isolated.

It is not necessary, I presume, to remind our readers of the beginnings of the Dublin struggle. Let us, just for convenience sake, take up the fight at the moment it became a subject of national action on the part of the British Labour movement.

A public meeting had been proclaimed in Dublin in a brazen illegal manner. For declaring that this proclamation was illegal, and advising their leaders to disregard it and stand to their rights, a number of leaders of the Irish Transport and General Workers' Union had been arrested and imprisoned. A wholesale batoning of the people had followed, and Dublin was the scene of the most unparalleled police brutality.

An appeal was made to the British Trades Union Congress, then happily sitting, and that body in the name of the British working class nobly rose to the occasion, and pledged the credit of the whole British labour movement to see their Dublin comrades through the fight. As a result, the right of free speech was re-asserted in Dublin, a supply of food was arranged for through the despatch of specially chartered steamers, and a huge amount of money was raised to enable the men and women of Dublin to keep the fight going. Never was seen such enthusiasm in a labour fight. Trade unionists, Socialists of all kinds, Anarchists, Industrialists, Syndicalists, all the varying and hitherto discordant elements of the Labour movement found a common platform, were joined together in pursuit of a common object. Now, permit me to underscore that point, and emphasise its great importance. For long years we have been preaching to the labour movement the necessity of concerted industrial action, telling it that the time was rotten ripe for Industrial Unity, and declaring that as the interests of each were the concern of all, our organisations should be rearranged with a view to the conserving of their common interests.

We found that to a large extent these ideas were taking root in the minds of the workers, but that to a still larger extent the tacit acceptance of our ideas failed to evoke concerted action built upon these lines. The forces of our enemies were united and wielded with all the precision and relentlessness with which the general staff of an army would wield the battalions and brigades which formed the component parts of that army, but the battalions and brigades of the army of labour when engaged in battle had no efficient general staff to guide and direct the whole army to the salvation of its individual units; and, worse still, had none of that esprit-de-corps which on the military battle-field would make the desertion of any section to its fate an unthinkable course to the officers of the divisions not engaged. We had seen at London, at Leith and elsewhere that whereas the whole force of the Shipping Federation has been actively engaged in fighting the dockers of these ports, the dockers and seamen of the other ports had maintained the peace, and left their Leith or London brothers to bear alone the full force of the Federation attack, instead of meeting that attack by a movement against the flanks and rear of the Federation in these other ports. We know that although much of this blundering was due to the sectional jealousy of various union leaders, much was also due to the fact that the conception of common action on a national scale by the whole working class had not yet entered the minds of the rank and file as a whole. Something had been wanting — something that would make the minds of the workers more responsive, more ready to accept the broader idea, and act upon its acceptance. That something Dublin supplied.

The dramatic suddenness with which the Dublin fight was thrust upon public attention, the tragic occurrences of the first few days — working class martyrdom, the happy coincidence of a Trade Union Congress, the intervention of British trade unionists to assert the right of public meeting for Irish workers — filling the gap in the ranks caused by the jailing of Irish Trade Union leaders, the brilliant inspiration of a food ship, and last but not least the splendid heroism of the Dublin men and women showing out against the background of the squalor and misery of their houses.

There are times in history when we realise that it is easier to convert a multitude than it ordinarily is to convert an individual; when indeed ideas seem to seize upon the masses as contra-distinguished by ordinary times when individuals slowly seize ideas. The propagandist toils on for decades in seeming failure and ignominy, when suddenly some great event takes place in accord with the principles he has been advocating, and immediately he finds that the seed he has been sowing is springing up in plants that are covering the earth. To the idea of working class unity, to the seed of industrial solidarity, Dublin was the great event that enabled it to seize the minds of the masses, the germinating force that gave power to the seed to fructify and cover these islands.

I say in all solemnity and seriousness that in its attitude towards Dublin the

Working Class Movement of Great Britain reached its highest point of moral grandeur — attained for a moment to a realisation of that sublime unity towards which the best in us must continually aspire. Could that feeling but have been crystallised into organic expression, could we but have had real statesmen amongst us who, recognising the wonderful leap forward of our class, would have hastened to burn behind us the boats that might make easy a retreat to the old ground of isolation and division, could we have found Labour Leaders capable enough to declare that now that the working class had found its collective soul it should hasten to express itself as befitted that soul and not be fettered by the rules, regulations and codes of organisations conceived in the olden outworn spirit of sectional jealousies; could these things have but been vouchsafed to us, what a new world could now be opening delightfully upon the vision of Labour? Consider what Dublin meant to you all! It meant that the whole force of organised Labour should stand behind each unit of organisation in each and all of its battles, that no company, battalion or brigade should henceforth be allowed to face the enemy alone, and that the capitalist would be taught that when he fought a Union anywhere he must be prepared to fight all Unions everywhere.

For the first days and weeks of the struggle, the Working Classes of Great Britain attained to the height of moral grandeur expressed in that idea, all Labour stood behind Dublin, and Dublin rejoiced. Dublin suffered and agonised, but rejoiced that even in its suffering it was the medium for the apostolate of a rejuvenating idea. How often have I heard the responsive cheers to the question whether they would be prepared to stand by others as these others had stood by them!

And now?

Dublin is isolated. We asked our friends of the transport trade unions to isolate the capitalist class of Dublin, and we asked the other unions to back them up. But no, they said we would rather help you by giving you funds. We argued that a strike is an attempt to stop the capitalist from carrying on his business, that the success or failure of the strike depends entirely upon the success or non-success of the capitalist to do without the strikers. If the capitalist is able to carry on his business without the strikers, then the strike is lost, even if the strikers receive more in strike pay than they formerly did in wages. We said that if scabs are working a ship and union men discharge in another port the boat so loaded, then those union men are strike breakers, since they help the capitalist in question to carry on his business. That if Union seamen man a boat discharged by scabs, these union seamen or firemen are by the same reason strike-breakers, as also are the railwaymen or carters who assist in transporting the goods handled by the scabs for the capitalist who is fighting his men or women. In other words, we appealed to the collective soul of the workers against the collective hatred of the capitalist.

We asked for no more than the logical development of that idea of working class unity, that the Working Class of Britain should help us to prevent the Dublin capitalists carrying on their business without us. We asked for the isolation of the capitalists of Dublin, and for answer the leaders of the British labour movement proceeded calmly to isolate the Working Class of Dublin. As an answer to those who supported our request for the isolation of Dublin we were told that a much better plan would be to increase the subsidies to enable us to increase strike pay. As soon as this argument had served its purpose, the subsidies fell off, and the "Dublin Fund" grew smaller and smaller as if by a pre-arranged plan. We had rejected the last terms offered by the employers on the strength of this talk of increased supplies, and as soon as that last attempt at settlement thus fell through, the supplies gradually froze up instead of being increased as we had been promised.

In addition to this the National Union of Railwaymen, whilst in attendance at the Special Conference in London on 9th December, had actually in their pockets the arrangements for the re-starting of work on the London and North-Western boat at the North Wall of Dublin, and in the train returning to Dublin the day after the Conference, we read of the line being re-opened. No vote was taken of the men on strike; they were simply ordered back to work by their officials and told that if they did not return, their strike pay would be stopped. The Seamen's and Firemen's Union men in Dublin were next ordered to man the boats of the Head Line of steamers then being discharged by free labourers supplied by the Shipping Federation. In both Dublin and Belfast the members refused, and they were then informed that union men would be brought from Great Britain to take their places. Union men to be brought from England to take the place of members of the same union who refused to desert their brothers of the Transport Union. We were attempting to hold up Guinness' porter. A consignment was sent to Sligo for shipment there. The local Transport Union official wired me for instructions. I wired to hold it up; his men obeyed, and it was removed from Sligo, railed to Derry, and there put on board by members of Mr Sexton's Union on ships manned by members of Mr Havelock Wilson's Union and discharged in Liverpool by members of Mr Sexton's Union. Whilst the City of Dublin Steam Packet Company was still insisting upon carrying the goods of our worst enemy, Jacob's (who is still enforcing the agreement denounced by Sir Geo. Askwith), the members of the Seamen and Firemen's Union were ordered to sign on in their boats, although our men were still on strike. We were informed by Mr. Joe Houghton of the Scottish Dockers that his Union would not hold up any boat for us unless joint action was taken by the Transport Workers' Federation. As on a previous occasion, his members at Ayr had worked coal boats belonging to a Belfast firm that was making war upon the Irish Transport Workers' Union, we do not blame Joe very much. He had been disobeyed at Ayr — perhaps he was coerced in Glasgow.

But why go on? Sufficient to say that the Working Class Unity of the first days of the Dublin fight was sacrificed in the interests of sectional officialism. The officials failed to grasp the opportunity offered to them to make a permanent reality of the Union of Working Class forces brought into being by the spectacle of rebellion, martyrdom and misery exhibited by the workers of Dublin. All England and Scotland rose to it; working class officialdom and working class rank and file alike responded to the call of inspiration; it would have raised us all upward and onward towards our common emancipation. But sectionalism, intrigues and old-time jealousies damned us in the hour of victory, and officialdom was the first to fall to the tempter.

And so we Irish workers must go down into Hell, bow our backs to the lash of the slave driver, let our hearts be seared by the iron of his hatred, and instead of the sacramental wafer of brotherhood and common sacrifice, eat the dust of defeat and betrayal.

Dublin is isolated.

• *Forward,* 7 February 1914

Executive of the Irish Trade Union Congress and Labour Party, 1914. James Connolly is standing on the left, Jim Larkin seated second from right.

We have fed you all for a thousand years

We have fed you all for a thousand years,
And you hail us still unfed.
Tho' there's never a dollar of all your wealth
But marks the workers' dead.

We have yielded our best to give you rest,
And you lie, self-fouled old bull;
For if blood be the price on all your wealth.
Good God, we have paid in full!

There's never a mine blown skyward now
But we're buried alive for you;
There's never a wreck drifts shore ward now
But we are its ghastly crew.

Go reckon our dead by the forges red,
And the factories where we spin;
If blood be the price of your cursed wealth
Good God, we have paid it in!

We have fed you all a thousand years.
For that was our doom, you know,
From the days when you chained us in your fields,
To the strike of a week ago.

You have eaten our lives and our babies and wives,
And we're told it's your legal share;
But if blood be the price of your lawful wealth,
Good God, we have bought it fair.

— Anonymous, early 20th century USA

The Problem of Trade Union Organisation

Recently I have been complaining in this column and elsewhere of the tendency in the Labour movement to mistake mere concentration upon the industrial field for essentially revolutionary advance. My point was that the amalgamation or federation of unions, unless carried out by men and women with the proper revolutionary spirit, was as likely to create new obstacles in the way of effective warfare, as to make that warfare possible. The argument was reinforced by citations of what is taking place in the ranks of the railwaymen and in the transport industry. There we find that the amalgamations and federations are rapidly becoming engines for steamrollering or suppressing all manifestations of revolutionary activity, or effective demonstrations of brotherhood. Every appeal to take industrial action on behalf of a union in distress is blocked by insisting upon the necessity of "first obtaining the sanction of the Executive", and in practice it is found that the process of obtaining that sanction is so long, so cumbrous, and surrounded with so many rules and regulations that the union in distress is certain to be either disrupted or bankrupted before the Executive can be moved. The Greater Unionism is found in short to be forging greater fetters for the working class; to bear to the real revolutionary industrial unionism the same relation as the servile State would bear to the Co-operative Commonwealth of our dreams.

This argument of mine, which to many people may appear as far-fetched, gains new strength from the circumstances related by our friend Robert Williams of the Transport Workers Federation, in the weekly report of that body for the 9 May. After describing how the Head Line Company played with the above Federation in connection with its protest against the continued victimisation of the members of the Irish Transport Workers' Union, and how he was *powerless* to effect anything as the other unions involved still continued to work the scab ships, he goes on to tell of a similar state of affairs in the Port of London. The quotation is long, but it is so valuable an instructive lesson to all your readers that I do not hesitate to give it as an ample confirmation of my argument.

"This week, again, there has been a recrudescence of the trouble existing be-

tween the Seamen's Union at Tilbury and the Anglo-American Oil Company. This Company has a fleet of oil-tank steamers running between America and various ports in this country.

"As a result of the protest made by the crew of the SS Narragansett against the chief steward, who acted in the most inhumane manner towards one of the crew who received a severe injury, this Company displaced union men and took on Shipping Federation scabs. Further than this, they have replaced all union men by obtaining Federation scabs in ship after ship since the commencement of the trouble. On Sunday last the Narragansett arrived once more at Purfleet, on the lower reaches of the Thames, and the Tilbury Secretary of the Seamen's Union, Mr E. Potton, naturally commenced to hustle. He communicated with Mr Harry Gosling, Mr Havelock Wilson, and the Secretary of this Federation, in order, if possible, to bring pressure upon the Company by preventing the ship from being bunkered.

"After consultation with Messrs Gosling and Wilson, the Secretary telephoned, and further, wrote the Anglo-American Oil Company asking them to confer with one or more of these three, in order to avoid a possible extension of the dispute to the 'coalies' and the tugboatmen, etc. (Purfleet steamers are bunkered from lighters). As in the case of the Head Line, the Secretary specifically drew the attention of the Anglo-American Oil Company to the nature of the complaints, and also sent a written request, following upon a telephone message, by a special messenger for the purpose of saving time. It should be remembered that the bunkers would all be aboard by Tuesday, and this was written on Monday. The Secretary was not very much surprised, however, to receive a reply asking him 'what exactly the complaints are, and on whose behalf they are made'. The reply was strangely in keeping with the replies received from the Head Line Company. The inference is that both these replies received inspiration from the same source.

"We are writing these words in the hope that they will be read by all those responsible for the guidance and control of the Transport Workers in all our seaports. On the face of it, it seems that the one course of action was to call off the men who were working on this ship. If the Company are asking for a fight, what earthly use is it to fight with a portion of your men, leaving all the others to render service to your enemy? This Company has made an open attack on all their employees who are members of the Seamen's Union. At the same time the cargo of oil was being pumped into reservoirs ashore by Trade Union engineers, the men employed ashore are members of an affiliated Union in the Federation, the ship is bunkered by members of an affiliated Union, the tugboats and lighters are staffed by members of an affiliated Union, and still

we are powerless.

"We are not so fatuous as to suggest that continuous warfare shall be waged by general strikes whenever a member considers he has a grievance, or whenever an official encounters a difficulty, but we feel that we are drifting back to the position we were in prior to 1911. A Federation with 29 Unions as its constituents, but with no ties more binding than the payment of 3d. per member per year, will not, and cannot, meet the requirements of modern industry. We are responsible to a quarter of a million men, and the existing methods are utterly incapable of protecting them from the insidious attacks of the employers. The organisation that is afraid of making a massed attack will experience a series of isolated disasters. The workers' organisation secures respect and consideration in proportion to the extent to which it can hamper and embarrass the employers against whom it is pitted.

"When co-operation is sought from one Union by another, the men involved say — Consult an official. The official says 'Get the consent of my E.C.'. The Executive officers say — 'Communicate with the Transport Workers' Federation'. The Federation waits on the decision of its own Executive, and by this inconsequent fiddling of time and opportunity, a thousand Romes would have burned to extinction.

"The employers move, strike, move, and strike again with the rapidity of a serpent, while we are turning about and contorting with the facility of an alligator. We have at once to determine whether the future is to mean for us efficiency, aptitude, capacity and life, or muddle, incompetence, decay and death".

Just what is the real remedy for this state of matters, it would be hard to say. But it is at least certain that the organisations I have been speaking of have not discovered the true methods of working-class organisations. They may be on the road to discovering it; they may also be on the road to foisting upon the working class a form of organisation which will make our last state infinitely worse than our first. It is the old story of adopting the letter but rejecting the spirit. The letter of industrial concentration is now accepted by all trade union officials, but the spirit of working-class solidarity is woefully absent. Each union and each branch of each union desires above all things to show a good balance sheet, and that that might be done every nerve is strained to keep their members at work, and in a condition to pay subscriptions. Hence the pitiful dodges to avoid taking sympathetic action in support of other unions, and hence also the constant victories of the master class upon the industrial field.

I have often thought that we of the working class are too slow, or too loath, to take advantage of the experience of our rulers. Perhaps if upon all questions of industrial or other war we followed more closely after them we would be able to fight them more successfully. Here is one suggestion I make on those lines. I am not welded to it, but I would like to see it discussed:

In the modern State the capitalist class has evolved for its own purposes of offence what it calls a Cabinet. This Cabinet controls its fighting forces, which must obey it implicitly. If the Cabinet thinks the time and opportunity is ripe for war, it declares war at the most favourable moment, and *explains its reasons in Parliament afterwards.*

Can we trust any of our members with such a weapon as the capitalist class trusts theirs? I think so. Can we not evolve a system of organisation which will leave to the unions the full local administration, but invest in a Cabinet the power to call out the members of any union when such action is desirable, and explain their reasons for it afterwards? Such a Cabinet might have the right to call upon all affiliated unions to reimburse the union whose members were called out in support of another, but such unions so supported would be under the necessity of obeying instantly the call of the Cabinet, or whatever might be the name of the board invested with the powers indicated.

Out of such an arrangement the way would be opened for a more thorough organisation of the working class upon the lines of real Industrial Unionism. At present we are too much afraid of each other. Whatever be our form of organisation, the spirit of sectionalism still rules and curses our class.

• *Forward*, 23 May 1914

"The Demon of Death" by Ernest Kavanagh, 6 September 1913 in The Irish Worker. *William Martin Murphy is depicted as a vulture at the gates of his estate, Dartry Hall.*

Old Wine in New Bottles

Scripture tells us in a very notable passage about the danger of putting new wine into old bottles. I propose to say a few words about the equally suicidal folly of putting old wine into new bottles. For I humbly submit that the experiment spoken of is very popular just now in the industrial world, has engaged the most earnest attention of most of the leaders of the working class, and received the practically unanimous endorsement of the Labour and Socialist Press. I have waited in vain for a word of protest.

In the year of grace 1905 a convention of American Labour bodies was held in Chicago for the purpose of promoting a new working-class organisation on more militant and scientific lines. The result of that convention was the establishment of the Industrial Workers of the World — the first Labour organisation to organise itself with the definite ideal of taking over and holding the economic machinery of society. The means proposed to that end — and it is necessary to remember that the form of organisation adopted was primarily intended to accomplish that end, and only in the second degree as a means of industrial warfare under capitalism — was the enrolment of the working class in Unions built upon the lines of the great industries. It was the idea of the promoters of the new organisation that craft interests and technical requirements should be met by the creation of branches, that all such branches should be represented in a common executive, that all united should be members of an industrial Union, which should embrace all branches and be co-extensive with the industry, that all industrial Unions should be linked as members of one great Union, and that one membership card should cover the whole working-class organisation. Thus was to be built up a working-class administration which should be capable of the revolutionary act of taking over society, and whose organisers and officers should in the preliminary stages of organising and fighting constantly remember, and remembering, teach, that no new order can replace the old until it is capable of performing the work of the old, and performing it more efficiently for human needs.

As one of the earliest organisers of that body, I desire to emphasise also that as a means of creating in the working class the frame of mind necessary to the upbuilding of this new order within the old, we taught, and I have yet seen no reason to reconsider our attitude upon this matter, that the interests of one were the interests of all, and that no consideration of a contract with a section of the capitalist class absolved any section of us from the duty of taking instant action to protect other sections when said sections were in danger from the capitalist enemy. Our attitude always was that in the swiftness and unexpectedness of our action lay our chief hopes of temporary victory, and since permanent peace was an illusory hope until permanent victory was secured, temporary victories were all that need concern us. We realised that every victory gained by the working class would be followed by some capitalist development that in course of time would tend to nullify it, but that until that development was perfect the fruits of our victory would be ours to enjoy, and the resultant moral effect would be of incalculable value to the character and to the mental attitude of our class towards their rulers. It will thus be seen that in our view — and now that I am about to point the moral I may personally appropriate it and call it my point of view — the spirit, the character, the militant spirit, the fighting character of the organisation, was of the first importance. I believe that the development of the fighting spirit is of more importance than the creation of the theoretically perfect organisation; that, indeed, the most theoretically perfect organisation may, because of its very perfection and vastness, be of the greatest possible danger to the revolutionary movement if it tends, or is used, to repress and curb the fighting spirit of comradeship in the rank and file.

Since the establishment in America of the organisation I have just sketched, and the initiation of propaganda on the lines necessary for its purpose, we have seen in all capitalist countries, and notably in Great Britain, great efforts being made to abolish sectional division, and to unite or amalgamate kindred Unions. Many instances will arise in the minds of my readers, but I propose to take as a concrete example the National Transport Workers' Federation. Previous to the formation of this body, Great Britain was the scene of the propagandist activities of a great number of irregular and unorthodox bodies, which, taking their cue in the main from the Industrial Workers of the World, made great campaigns in favour of the new idea. Naturally their arguments were in the main directed towards emphasising the absurdity implied in one body of workers remaining at work whilst another body of workers were on strike in the same employment. As a result of this campaign, frowned upon by leading officials in Great Britain, the Seamen's strike of 1911 was conducted on, and resulted in, entirely new lines of action. The sympathetic strike sprang into being; every group of workers stood by every allied group of workers; and a great wave of effective solidarity caught the workers in its grasp and beat and terrified the masters. Let me emphasise the point that the greatest weapon against capital was proven in those days to be the sporadic strike. It was its very sporadic nature, its swiftness and unexpectedness, that won. It was ambush, the surprise attack of our industrial army, before which the well-trained battalions of the capitalist crumpled up in panic, against which no precautions were available.

Since that time we have had all over these countries a great wave of enthusiasm for amalgamations, for more cohesion in the working-class organisations. In the transport industry all Unions are being linked up until the numbers now affiliated have become imposing enough to awe the casual reader and silence the cavilling objector at Trade Union meetings. But I humbly submit that, side by side with that enlargement and affiliation of organisations, there has proceeded a freezing up of the fraternal spirit of 1911; there is now, despite the amalgamations, less solidarity in the ranks of Labour than was exhibited in that year of conflict and victory.

If I could venture an analysis of the reason for this falling-off in solidarity, I would have to point out that the amalgamations and federations are being carried out in the main by officials absolutely destitute of the revolutionary spirit, and that as a consequence the methods of what should be militant organisations having the broad working-class outlook are conceived and enforced in the temper and spirit of the sectionalism those organisations were meant to destroy.

Into the new bottles of industrial organisation is being poured the old, cold wine of Craft Unionism.

The much-condemned small Unions of the past had at least this to recommend them, viz., that they were susceptible to pressure from the sudden fraternal impulses of their small membership. If their members worked side by side with scabs, or received tainted goods from places where scabs were employed, the shame was all their own, and proved frequently too great to be borne. When it did so we had the sympathetic strike and the fraternisation of the working class. But when the workers handling tainted goods, or working vessels loaded by scabs, are members of a nation-wide organisation, with branches in all great centres or ports, the sense of the personal responsibility is taken off the shoulders of each member and local officials, and the spirit of solidarity destroyed. The local official can conscientiously order the local member to remain at work with the scab, or to handle the tainted goods, "pending action by the General Executive".

As the General Executive cannot take action pending a meeting of delegates, and as the delegates at that meeting have to report back to their bodies, and these bodies again to meet, discuss, and then report back to the General Executive, which must meet, hear their reports, and then, perhaps, order a ballot vote of the entire membership, after which another meeting must be held to tabulate the result of the vote and transmit it to the local branches, which must meet again to receive it, the chances are, of course, a million to one that the body of workers in distress will be starved into subjection, bankrupted, or disrupted, before the leviathan organisation will allow their brothers on the spot to lift a finger or drop a tool in their aid. Readers may, perhaps, think that I am exaggerating the danger. But who will think so that remembers the vindictive fine imposed by the NUR upon its members in the North of England for taking swift action on behalf of a persecuted comrade instead of going through all this red tape whilst he was suffering? Or who will think so that knows that Dublin and Belfast members of the Irish Transport Workers' Union have been victimised ever since the end of the lock-out by the Head Line Company, whose steamers have been and are regularly coaled in British ports, and manned by Belfast and British members of the Seamen's and Firemen's Union?

The amalgamations and federations that are being built up today are, without exception, being used in the old spirit of the worst type of sectionalism; each local Union or branch finds in the greater organisation of which it is a part a shield and excuse for refusing to respond to the call of brothers and sisters in distress, for the handling of tainted goods, for the working of scab boats. A main reason for this shameful distortion of the Greater Unionism from its true purpose is to be found in the campaign against "sporadic strikes". I have no doubt but that Robert Williams, of the National Transport Workers' Federation, is fully convinced that his articles and speeches against such strikes are and were wise; I have just as little doubt that they were the best service performed for the capitalist by any Labour leader of late years. The big strike, the vast massed battalions of Labour against the massed battalions of capital on a field every inch of which has been explored and mapped out beforehand, is seldom successful, for very obvious reasons. The sudden strike, and the sudden threat to strike suddenly, has won more for Labour than all the great Labour conflicts in history. In the Boer war the long line of communications was the weak point of the British army; in a Labour war the ground to be covered by the goods of the capitalist is his line of communication. The larger it is the better for the attacking forces of Labour. But these forces must be free to attack or refuse to attack, just as their local knowledge guides them. But, it will be argued, their action might imperil the whole organisation. Exactly so, and their inaction might imperil that working-class spirit which is more important than any organisation. Between the horns of that dilemma what can be done? In my opinion, we must recognise that the only solution of that problem is the choice of officers, local or national, from the standpoint of their responsiveness to the call for solidarity, and, having got such officials, to retain them only as long as they can show results in the amelioration of the condition of their members and the development of their Union as a weapon of class warfare.

If we develop on those lines, then the creation of a great Industrial Union, such as I have rudely sketched in my opening reminiscence, or the creation of those much more clumsy federations and amalgamations now being formed, will be of immense revolutionary value to the working class; if, on the contrary, we allow officialism of the old, narrow sectional kind to infuse their spirit into the new organisations, and to strangle these with rules suited only to a somnolent working class, then the Greater Unionism will but serve to load us with great fetters. It will but be to real Unionism what the Servile State would be to our ideal Co-operative Commonwealth.

• *The Age*, 30 April 1914

Crowds in Dublin await food ships from England, during the Dublin Labour War

William Orpen's illustration of a Liberty Hall soup kitchen during the Dublin Labour War

A Lesson of the Strike

The long-drawn out fight with the City of Dublin Steam Packet Company is one of the most striking lessons yet offered of the absurdity of our present social arrangements. Here we have the spectacle of one man being able to upset the business and destroy the happiness of a whole community, in order to gratify his personal spleen against men who refused to be lowered beneath the level of their fellows. We find the Chamber of Commerce, representing all their fellow-business men; the Lord Mayor, representing the interests of the city at large; the Under Secretary for Ireland, representing the British Government in Dublin; and the Chief Industrial Commissioner, Sir George Askwith, representing the Government of Great Britain, all anxious to have the dispute settled and the business of the port resumed. And this one man is able to set them all at defiance, and proceed on his own way, wrecking their hopes along with his own business.

The social system we live under is held by its apologists to be the one that gives the greatest freedom to the individual, combined with the fullest service to the community.

The work of serving the public is not undertaken by a public authority but is left to the haphazard enterprise of individuals spurred by the desire of gain. People are not fed, clothed, housed, or warmed because the feeding, clothing, housing or warming is a public duty; but because certain individuals think that they can make a profit by so doing. If at any time these individuals think that they are not making enough profit by performing these functions, then they cease rendering this public service, and the whole life of the community is thrown out of gear. This dispute is a case in point. Every shipowner on the quays of Dublin has learned that he can pay the rate of wages asked by the City of Dublin Company strikers, and make a profit while doing so. Knowing this to be the case they keep their boats running to serve themselves and the public. The Chairman of the City of Dublin Steam Packet Company declares that he cannot make his boats pay under the same conditions as his competitors, and stops his boats accordingly. If his statement is true then it is a most lamentable confession of inefficiency and bungling mismanagement. Yet no power says to this man –

Either run your boats, or resign and go out of business. You cannot be allowed to disarrange the business of half of the merchants in the city.

He as owner of the mail boat from Kingstown receives a large Government subsidy, and is thus in a better position than his competitors who have to make their business pay without any such aid. If he cannot make his business pay then he should be treated as he would treat a dock labourer who could not work under the same conditions as his fellows — he should be fired to make room for men who can.

But just there is the weakness of the present social system. His is not a public service, and he is not a public servant. It is a private service for private gain, and he is a private individual out for private profit, and willing to punish all his associates in the business world in order to make that profit — or in revenge for not making a profit big enough.

Some day the world will wake up sufficiently to recognise that the capitalist conducting business on his own account is just as much a nuisance, and as bunglingly inefficient at the job, as were the soldier chiefs of the past making war on their own account. And when the world does so recognise the fact it will reduce private business enterprises to the same level as private armies and private wars. The nation will take over the work of organising the industries of peace as it has taken out of private hands the owning of armies and the conducting of wars for private profit.

And when it thinks about that matter the recollection of the City of Dublin Steam Packet Company's war upon the interests of the port of Dublin will be of great service in educating the public mind to agree to the change.

• *Workers' Republic*, 8 January 1916

The Immigrant

Recently standing in the railroad depot at Youngstown, Ohio, waiting for a train I witnessed a spectacle that called up in my old heart some very deep emotions.

As a train from the West pulled into the depot there alighted from it an Italian peasant woman and five little children, all dressed in the characteristic garb of the Italian peasants. In about a half hour, another train drawing in, they were hurried aboard, and as they scrambled up the steps the old mother ran from one to the other gathering them under her care "as a hen gathereth her chicks".

To me the solicitude and anxiety of the old woman was deeply touching; cast upon the stormy waters of American life, more than three thousand miles from home, and knowing not a word of the language spoken around her, she was evidently absorbed in the one great thought of protecting and caring, at all risks to herself, for her little ones.

But to the majority of the lookers-on there the spectacle apparently excited only derision, and some of the most openly derisive laughter came from the American women and girls with whom the platform was crowded.

These things set me thinking, and speculating, and to my mind's eye there came the vision of that great army of proletarian women of whom that poor peasant woman was no unworthy sample.

I could not see the uncouthness, and the rude garb, and the clumsy shoes, and all the other marks of poverty and unrequited toil which hypnotised the giggling womenkind around me: I could only see the love and unselfishness and abiding faith exemplified in that poor member of my class in her venture upon the cold world of Capitalist America. Looking beneath the surface of things I could see some poor, despised, un-skilled Italian labourer in some of our construction gangs in town or country, toiling under the eyes of a harsh unfeeling boss, sleeping at night in a rude, uncomfortable, unhealthy slum or shack, living on the poorest and cheapest food, and all the time scraping every cent together with his thoughts fixed upon the wife and children he had left thousands of miles away.

And I could picture that trusting wife and those innocent children waiting for long weary months upon some Piedmontese hillside, in the malarial wastes of the Roman Campagna, amid the quarries of Sicily, or the uncharted labyrinths of Calabria — waiting, waiting, waiting in penury and suffering and anguish and hunger, waiting until the husband and father would send the American dollars — sanctified with his sweat and blood — to redeem them and bring them to the new land of promise.

And then I could see that poor ignorant woman, poor in this world's wealth, but how rich in faith and love — rise up out of her old home, tear herself away from all the associations and sweet memories of her childhood, and gathering around her her little babies, set out with them upon that three or four thousand mile travel across sea and land, amid hostile and unsympathetic strangers, to rejoin her husband and sacrifice herself to make a home for her children.

Talk of the faith that inspired the Crusades. What was it in comparison with that faith shown by these European wives and mothers, who, in every land in Europe, are year in and year out, paralleling the experiences of that poor Italian peasant?

In Italy, in Russia, in Poland, in Germany, in Scandinavia, in Turkey, in Hungary, aye in all the countries of the Old World that new Crusade is taking place, the poor women of the propertyless classes are waiting and suffering and hoping and achieving.

And it is these people who bring to this country such rich stores of faith, affection, and capabilities of patient martyrdom for their children that some political and social quacks would brand as undesirable aliens, as backward races.

Think of it! And think also of the thousands of instances in which all that martyrdom, all that travail of emigration and breaking of home ties, brought no relief to the sufferers, brought them only from the companionship and human sympathy of the old world to the cruel unfeeling environment of a new world mad for gold, of a world basing all its activities and relations upon a "cash nexus", upon a calculation centring round the dollar.

Yet this crusade, this martyrdom of the poor, must go on until Capitalism is crushed out and Socialism is achieved. Until then the plaintive sorrowing verses of our Irish poetess, Ethna Carberry, will remain an epitome of, and a fitting dirge to the dispersion not only of our Irish peasantry, but to those of all Europe.

They are going, going, going from the valleys and the hills,
They are leaving far behind them heathery moor and mountain rills,
All the wealth of hawthorn hedges, where the brown thrush sways and trills!

They are going, shy-eyed colleens, and lads so straight and tall,
From the purple peaks of Kerry, from the crags of wild Imael,
From the greening plains of Mayo, and the glens of Donegal.

So some must wander to the East, and some must wander West,
Some seek the white wastes of the North, and some a Southern nest,
Yet never shall they sleep so sweet as on your mother's breast.

Within the city streets, hot, hurried, full of care,
A sudden dream shall bring them a whiff of Irish air —
A cool air faintly scented, blown soft from otherwhere.

They may win a golden store — sure the whins were golden too,
And no foreign skies hold beauty like the rainy skies they knew,
Nor any night wind cool the brow as did the foggy dew.

• From "Harp Strings", *The Harp*, January 1909

Cartoon by Ernest Kavanagh in 1913, showing what the Labour War revealed

Timeline of 1913-14 Labour War

July: Murphy tells tram workers he will sack them unless they disavow ITGWU

August 26: Workers stop all trams, in protest and to seek pay rises

August 29-31: Police riot, attacking workers' demonstrations

September 1: British TUC congress pledges support

September: Employers extend lock-out

September 9: Connolly goes on a hunger strike in jail, which will win his release; Larkin goes to England for a fundraising tour

Mid-September: Unofficial action by railworkers and others, refusing to handle goods from Dublin

September 27: First of several ships organised by British trade unions arrives in Dublin with food aid for the Dublin workers

October 5: A Board of Trade inquiry recommends peace terms which the union accepts as a basis for negotiations, but the bosses flatly reject

October 6: Miners' Federation conference in Britain calls for general strike in solidarity

October 18: Dora Montefiore and others begin to organise to have strikers' children billeted with supporters' families in England and Northern Ireland for duration of dispute. Catholic priests denounce and obstruct

October 28: Connolly becomes acting general secretary of union while Larkin is jailed

November 1: Giant rally at Albert Hall in London in solidarity with strike, called by Daily Herald

Mid-November: Renewed rank and file solidarity action in Britain. Larkin does speaking tour in Britain

December 4: TUC leaders visit Dublin to seek new talks, which again fail because bosses refuse all compromise

December 9: TUC special conference votes down motion for comprehensive boycott of goods from lockout employers. Support from British unions starts to scale down

January: Irish Labour Party (formed by trade unions in 1912) makes its first election campaign, with candidates in Dublin municipal elections

January 15: Labour candidates narrowly fail to win more than one seat in Dublin municipal elections

January 19: Larkin advises strikers to go back to work on the best terms they can get. Over the following weeks the strike gradually ebbs.

WHAT TIME IS IT?

JOIN THE I.W.W.

WAKE UP!
LONG HOURS
POVERTY
WAGE SLAVERY
JOIN the I.W.W.

THE I.W.W. is COMING!
JOIN THE ONE BIG UNION